Circle of Catholic Women

~ *journal one* ~

*personal reflection and group sharing
to help you deepen your faith and
find balance in your everyday life*

~

Karen Pavlicin

Julota
celebrating life

✤ ✤ ✤ ✤ ✤ ✤ ✤ ✤ ✤
Woodbury, Minnesota

Juloya is an imprint of Elva Resa Publishing
8362 Tamarack Vlg Ste 119-106, St Paul, MN 55125
http://www.juloya.com, http://www.elvaresa.com
http://www.circleofcatholicwomen.com

Circle of Catholic Women journals are available through traditional bookstores, online, or direct from the publisher. Bulk discounts available. A portion of profits supports outreach programs for women, children, and families.

To the circle of women in my life

Journal One

Introduction

How this journal series began...in a circle of women...
Participating in a women's group can change your life. It changed mine.
One spring I signed up for a journaling program for moms. About a
dozen women—many of us began as strangers—met each week for
twelve weeks. We read scripture, journaled about our lives, and shared
personal stories and beliefs. Some women were in the midst of
transitioning from working full time to staying at home with young
children. Some had suffered recent losses: loved ones who died, job
layoffs, struggling relationships. A few were healing from other life-
changing events. Some were in a great place in their lives. We had
women who were new moms, single moms, young and old, all looking
for a deeper connection with God, fellowship with other spiritual
women, and a way to formally give time and attention to their own
needs as women and mothers.

When we finished our session, we wanted more. So we began a book
study group. Each week we read a chapter in the book and talked about
how our faith affected our daily lives. Still, we wanted more. It seemed
the more we met, the closer the friendships, the deeper our faith, and
the more easily we began to see our faith manifested in mornings with

our children and other aspects of life. It also increased our desire to do more for our community. We formed a women's ministry focused on fellowship, faith sharing, and outreach. Our group soon expanded to include many women from all walks of life, all wanting to hear from and share with other women our real-life experiences and challenges. We wanted to inspire each other to deepen our faith and support each other as we put our spirituality to work in all aspects of our lives. That desire is what initiated this journal series.

A series of journals

The *Circle of Catholic Women* program is a series of journals. Each journal has a similar format to other journals in the series, with eight chapters (seven topics and one reflection). The series is non-sequential so you can start with any journal in the series. The format allows an individual or group flexibility for participating and offers some variety season to season for those who attend multiple or consecutive sessions.

In *Journal One*, we reflect on our communication with God through prayer as well as listening to how he is calling us to serve. We share our recognition of Jesus in others and ways we pass along special celebrations of his love. We also consider how our faith plays out in our personal lifestyle decisions, especially ways we use our financial gifts and ways our body and soul can feed each other for a balanced lifestyle.

The journal topics are presented within the context of the Catholic faith. You could discuss these topics based on any religion. But as Catholic women we wanted to better understand what the Catholic Church was asking us to believe.

Having the Church (or anyone else) tell you what to believe is not what creates belief. Life experiences—both joyful and sad, divine messages, relationships with the people around you, being faced with decisions that go in a direction other than the teachings—that is what strengthens faith and defines your beliefs. So while there are references to what the Church believes, I encourage you to question how that belief plays out in your life. It doesn't mean you'll pick and choose which beliefs you'll call your own, but it does mean you'll look deeper to understand why you believe and how that belief affects your thoughts and actions.

For example, the Catholic Church believes there is a heaven, an afterlife. My husband, Bob, died of cancer at age 38. If someone had asked me about heaven before he died, I would have said, sure I believe in heaven. But it didn't go much deeper than that thought. After Bob died, I had all sorts of questions about heaven and what I really believed. Could he see me? Hear me? Intervene on my behalf? Was he watching our child grow? Does time exist in heaven? Does every good and decent person go there? Would we still be married in heaven? Suddenly, I needed to go much deeper in my faith than simply believing in an afterlife.

In the same way, I began to reflect on other areas of my faith. Not because I didn't believe, but because I wanted to better understand what I did believe. The questions in this journal might prompt you to ask about official Church teachings, talk with your priest, read more about the topic in the Bible, seek out the perspective of other women, or reevaluate how you live your faith. Many discussions won't have a right answer. Explore the deeper, uncomfortable level. Honest, personal reflection is part of what helps us better understand our faith in the context of everyday life, so we can put our trust in God and respond to his call.

How to use this journal

Circle of Catholic Women is designed to prompt journaling and reflection by individual women, followed by sharing and discussion in a group setting. The purpose is to deepen your understanding of your faith and build fellowship with other women as you inspire each other to live your faith in all aspects of your daily lives.

Your circle of women can choose to use the journal in a variety of settings. For example, you can select two journal topics for a half-day retreat, four topics for a month-long weekly series, or the entire journal in an eight-week session, with a weekly meeting on the same day and time each week.

For the most meaningful group discussions, each person should read and journal about the topic before the group meeting.

Tips for personal journaling
Find a time and place where you can read and reflect with few interruptions. If you try to read the night before your meeting while helping a child with homework or watching a television show, you are cheating yourself of time for you. Make two or three appointments with yourself during the week for quiet reflective time. Don't try to complete the whole week's journey in one sitting. Questions are grouped together so you can reflect on and write about one portion of the week's topic at a time.

Be honest with yourself when you answer questions. Know that whatever you journal about, you have a choice whether or not you want to share it with the group. When you are going through the topics the first time, it is for your own understanding of your beliefs, your questions, and your desires. Don't think about or worry about group sharing when you are doing your personal journaling.

Feel free to use the margins to answer different questions if you feel moved to talk about the topic in a different way. The journal prompts are there only to help you think about different aspects of the topic. You do not have to answer all of them. Write about what moves you, what you have questions about, what frustrates you or causes you to more deeply reflect on the impact of your faith on your daily life.

When meeting as a group
This journaling program is flexible to allow a group to share with or without a facilitator. A few suggestions:

If possible, meet as a group before you begin the program, for example, the week before an eight-week session. Introduce each other. Use ice breakers to help everyone learn a little about each other. Hand out the books and talk about the format of the program, how the group will be facilitated, the schedule, and general expectations. Answer questions. Help everyone feel comfortable that this will be a personally rewarding experience in an environment of compassionate trust.

For each meeting, create an atmosphere that encourages spiritual connections. Sit in a circle or around a table where each person can see the others. Light a candle. Consider setting the table with an object related to the day's discussion topic. Minimize distractions by closing the door to the room, moving children to a childcare room, and turning off cell phones.

Open with a prayer, poem, or music. You can use the opening provided in the journal or use a passage, poem, or song brought in by a member of your group.

Agree that you will not share someone else's personal story outside the circle unless you have that person's permission. By keeping personal stories within this trusted circle, you provide a safe place for everyone to share and grow.

As you go through the journal together, don't feel you need to discuss every question. Often personal stories will be reflected over a set of questions. One way to open up the discussion is to share overall feelings about the topic you reflected on and wrote about that week. Did the topic evoke any strong feelings? Was it comfortable or difficult for you? Are there any questions you especially want to talk about or hear from other women about? At the end of each chapter are suggested group discussion questions. As you journal, if there is a topic or question you especially want to discuss, make a note in the group discussion section.

If, during your group discussion, a topic or set of questions takes you on a tangent, go with it. Let the Spirit guide you. Sometimes those side conversations are rich with personal experience and divine messages. Decide beforehand how your group prefers to transition from these side discussions, such as assigning a time keeper who can gently bring you back to the main topic at an appropriate time.

Depending on the number of women in your circle, try splitting up the group into small groups of two to seven women for part of the meeting. Sharing responses in more intimate small-group or one-on-one conversations allows more women to share with each other and to develop close relationships. Use creative ways to randomly select small groups, such as drawing Uno cards and gathering in tables by card color. When you come back together in the larger group, you can volunteer to share comments that your small group felt might benefit everyone to hear.

Keep to the amount of time your group has agreed to allot for the meeting. Our group meets for 1-1/2 hours. Having a set amount of time shows respect for the commitment you've each shown to make this circle a priority in your busy schedules. It also helps you plan out enough time to talk about the aspects of the week's topic you really want to share.

Leave a few minutes at the end of each gathering to share resources and get feedback on how the sessions are going. Close with a prayer.

To encourage friendships within the circle, set up ways for women to connect before, during, after, and in between meetings. For example, at each meeting, have a theme for name tags; ask each person to write a favorite movie, book, or hobby on her name tag and sit near someone with similar or opposite favorites. Sit next to a different person each time you meet. Draw names after each meeting and later in the week call the person whose name you drew.

Tips for facilitators

Decide ahead of time how your group discussions will be facilitated. Depending on the size of your group, the personalities of your participants, and your meeting surroundings, you might prefer to have a primary facilitator who organizes the meetings and leads the discussions. You might need a team of facilitators to lead several small group discussions. Or your group might prefer to have different volunteers sign up to facilitate each week or to have no formal facilitator. If you want facilitation guidance beyond the suggested questions at the end of each chapter, please see the separate facilitator guide for this journal. (*Circle of Catholic Women—Journal One: Facilitator Guide* includes a step-by-step plan for setting up your circle program and leading the meetings for each topic; additional options and summary questions for the final reflections chapter; and retreat ideas.) Whichever method of facilitation you choose, explain the process to your group ahead of time so everyone understands and is comfortable with the approach. In general, facilitators will want to:

- Be prepared. Complete your own journaling and look over the discussion questions ahead of time.

- Set a positive and welcoming tone. Encourage everyone to let go of their distractions or other worries so they can fully engage in the present discussion. Invite all participants to share their experiences, thoughts, and questions. Help each person feel welcomed and encouraged to participate but not pressured.

- Review the guidelines for meeting as a group, such as keeping conversations confidential within the group in order to create a trusted environment. Ask everyone to be mindful that all sharing is personal and that each story should be honored and respected.

- Help keep the group reasonably on topic and on time. Guide the discussion and timing to cover all topics your group is expecting to talk about within the overall allotted time. If the discussion takes a slight tangent, go with it and see where the Spirit guides you. At the appropriate time, gently refocus the group back on topic.

- Listen without judgment. Remind participants that you aren't here to solve each other's problems, but to let each woman be heard who wants to share and to provide a supportive environment for that sharing. It's okay to acknowledge someone's joy or pain, but avoid advice or opinions. Listening is as important as being heard. Be open to silence. Be open to truly listening in a way that you may reflect on it later for your own growth and learning.

- If one person dominates a conversation or has trouble bringing her thoughts to closure, gently thank her for sharing and explain that due to time constraints, you'd like to invite others to share. As facilitator, remember that it is not your role to dominate either; you are there to guide the discussion and allow everyone who wants to share to have the opportunity to do so.

- Keep the conversation inspirational and respectful. Recognize that some topics will be fun while others may generate deep emotions. Be aware of times when someone may need a moment to collect her thoughts or composure. As facilitator, be sensitive to the potential need for a short break.

- About ten minutes before closing, let participants know that you are near the end of the discussion time. Guide the group toward last reflections or comments before closing with a prayer. Thank everyone for participating and encourage them to reflect on this time spent together before beginning the next journal topic.

- Be open to suggestions for changes to the format or facilitation. What works well for one group may be different from what works for another.

Personal reflection following the group meeting

At the end of each chapter is a set of questions to encourage further reflection. After you've discussed the topic as a group and before you begin journaling about the next topic, take some time to reflect on what you experienced. How did the group's discussion and your own journaling move you? At the end of the journal, there is an opportunity to reflect on your overall experience and to discuss as a group anything you want to share from your weekly reflections. This reflection time is often the most important for women. It's the time when you begin to understand how the Spirit is guiding you through this experience, a time when you can purposely assess where you are on your spiritual path and how you can bring your faith into action in your daily lives.

The labyrinth

The cover of each journal incorporates a labyrinth; at the center is a circle, a special place of reflection and renewal. Walking a labyrinth is a journey of self-awareness, enlightenment, and peace. Unlike the maze of our daily lives with all its choices and unexpected turns, a labyrinth has only one path to the center and back. It allows us to completely focus and meditate and find our own center. There is something unique and sacred about being at the center of a labyrinth:

> "To enter the center of the labyrinth is to enter the belly of the soul where the darkness illuminates the light."
> *Book of Reflections*, the guest book of the Labyrinth Project of Connecticut

Whether we walk it on our own or with others, there is a blessing in perspective gained:

> "I walked the labyrinth feeling others' joy and sadness as well as my own, and understanding that I didn't have to fix the others' pain or add to their joy, only validate and allow their feelings." *Book of Reflections*

My hope is that your experience within your circle of women will be similar to walking a labyrinth.

May God bless you on this journey!

connecting with god

Personal Prayer Practices

Light a candle

Opening prayer

Lord and Father, teach me to talk with you openly and honestly. Sometimes I am afraid to ask for what I truly need or to tell you how I really feel. You see and know all things. You know my thoughts and my heart's desires. Help me be patient and trust you. Grant not always what I ask but according to your plan, for I can only see what is in front of me in my own life. You see all life now and forever. Help me know that you hear my prayers whether your answer is "no" or "not now" or "yes, but not in the way you expected" or "I thought you'd never ask." I know you love me. I love you, too. Teach me how to do your will, how to make you proud of me, how to show my love for you, how to make the time for us to meet and chat so I can learn from your wisdom. I will listen when you speak. Amen.

"Pray without ceasing." 1 Thessalonians 5:17 NAB

"Prayer and Christian life are inseparable."
Catechism of the Catholic Church (2757)

The power of prayer has overcome enemies (Psalm 6:9-10), conquered death (2 Kings 4:3-36), brought healing (James 5:14-15), and defeated demons (Mark 9:25-29). God, through prayer, opens eyes, changes hearts, heals wounds, and grants wisdom (James 1:5). No wonder we want to know how to pray!

What is prayer?

> "Only when we humbly acknowledge that 'we do not know how to pray as we ought,' (Romans 8: 26) are we ready to receive freely the gift of prayer."
> *Catechism of the Catholic Church* (2559)

Prayer comes in many forms. There are physical forms of prayer, such as genuflection, making the sign of the cross, kneeling, and fasting. Jesus gave us the wonderful Lord's prayer in Matthew 6:9-13:

> "This is how you are to pray: 'Our Father in heaven, hallowed be your name, your kingdom come, your will be done, on earth as in heaven. Give us today our daily bread; and forgive us our debts, as we forgive our debtors; and do not subject us to the final test, but deliver us from the evil one.'" NAB

What a loving example of how to pray and what to pray about: worship, trust in God, requests, confession, protection. He loves it just as much when we pray our own words.

> "The Lord delights in any time we spend in His presence whether we are speaking words of one favorite prayer or quietly listening." —Father Tom Walker

What is prayer to you? Do you offer praise or petitions, or do you have a conversation with God? Think about how you pray, including what you say and how you listen for God's response. How does prayer bring you closer in your personal relationship with God?

As you reflect on your beliefs about prayer, consider its role in your personal connection with God the Father, the Son, and the Holy Spirit.

Right now in my life, prayer means:

_____

_____

_____

What I wonder about how other people pray:

_____

_____

_____

"The Christian family is the first place for education in prayer." *Catechism of the Catholic Church* (2694)

What do I teach my children about prayer?

_____

_____

_____

What do my children teach me about prayer?

_____

_____

_____

Stacy kneels with her children each night at the side of their beds and teaches them favorite prayers to recite and how to create their own prayers to God.

13

Conversations with God

"Persevere in prayer, being watchful in it with thanksgiving."
Colossians 4:2 NAB

"Prayer of praise is entirely disinterested and rises to God,
lauds him, and gives him glory for his own sake, quite
beyond what he has done, but simply because HE IS."
Catechism of the Catholic Church (2649)

What are my personal prayer practices?

---

*Each morning in
the shower, Katie
prays: "Lord, may
your Word and
Spirit cleanse my
heart and mind."*

When I pray, do I think of God as my Father? Do I pray to
Jesus? To the Holy Spirit?

When do I hear God speaking to me?

When is it most difficult for me to hear God?

How does my personal prayer help me know God better? What do I learn from God through prayer?

_____

_____

_____

How is praying similar to having tea with a new acquaintance or an old friend? Talking with a parent or grandparent? Receiving guidance from a spiritual director?

_____

_____

_____

Kira prays in the little moments of the day...while folding laundry, going for a walk, making dinner. "It's like being with a good friend all day long."

Messages in my life I believe came directly from God (Father, Son, or Spirit):

_____

_____

_____

How I received those messages:

_____

_____

_____

What I love about my conversations with God:

_____

_____

_____

15

What frustrates me about my conversations with God:

_____

_____

Are there times I ask someone else to talk with God for me? A saint in heaven? A loved one who passed away? Someone in my life on earth? How is this different from talking with God directly?

_____

_____

_____

Why is prayer sometimes difficult?

"The habitual difficulty in prayer is distraction… To set about hunting down distractions would be to fall into their trap, when all that is necessary is to turn back to our heart: for a distraction reveals to us what we are attached to, and this humble awareness before the Lord should awaken our preferential love for him and lead us resolutely to offer him our heart to be purified. Therein lies the battle, the choice of which master to serve." *Catechism of the Catholic Church* (2729)

What distractions keep me from intimate prayer?

Megan is easily distracted by daily chores and her young children. She feels the most joy in spontaneous personal prayer.

_____

_____

_____

When do I find it most difficult to pray?

_____

When is it easiest for me to pray?

_____

_____

_____

God answers prayers

"Ask and it will be given to you; seek and you will find; knock and the door will be opened to you. For everyone who asks, receives; and the one who seeks, finds; and to the one who knocks, the door will be opened." Matthew 7:7-8 NAB

"Therefore I tell you, all that you ask for in prayer, believe that you will receive it and it shall be yours." Mark 11:24 NAB

"'Faith is being sure of what we hope for and certain of what we do not see' (Hebrews 11:1). True faith relies on God and believes before seeing. Naturally, we want some evidence that our petition is granted before we believe, but when we 'live by faith' (2 Cor. 5:7), we need no evidence other than God's word. He has spoken, and in harmony with our faith it will be done. We will see because we have believed, and true faith sustains us in the most trying of times, even when everything around us seems to contradict God's word."
—*Life of Praise / Streams in the Desert*

A time God answered my prayer (even if it wasn't what I expected) and how I felt about it:

_____

_____

_____

_____

_____

A time when I was angry or upset with God or with the way I thought he answered my prayer:

*Does my belief
and trust in God
affect his answer?
Does his answer
affect my trust and
belief in him?*

A time when I felt God was not going to answer my prayer in the way I wanted him to yet I asked anyway:

This is what I believe about how God answers prayers:

Praying for others

"Prayer of intercession consists in asking on behalf of another. It knows no boundaries and extends to one's enemies." *Catechism of the Catholic Church* (2647)

Sometimes our personal prayers are for someone else, perhaps a loved one in trouble or someone less fortunate than ourselves. They can be for someone we don't know, such as saying a "Hail Mary" when hearing an ambulance siren or a simple "God bless the rescue heroes and the people they are rescuing."

We can and should pray for our "enemies" as well: a coworker we don't like, a bully at school, a neighbor who doesn't share our values, a thief or criminal in our community, a terrorist.

How do I pray for others? What words do I use with God when praying for someone else?

How do I decide who is on my personal prayer list? Do I share with those people that I'm praying for them, or do I pray silently?

How is praying for someone else different from my other prayers?

Under what circumstances is it difficult to pray for someone else?

What I believe about petitions and intercessions:

"For where two or three are gathered together in my name, there am I in the midst of them." Matthew 18:20 NAB

Many parishes offer a prayer book. Imagine an entire congregation praying for your family.

*When Julia's mom
was sick, her parish
and friends prayed for
her mother's recovery.
"It was so powerful
to know we weren't
alone in asking
God for healing."*

How I feel when someone prays for me or on my behalf:

....

....

How I feel when I pray for others:

....

....

Why is prayer necessary?

"And when you pray, do not keep on babbling like pagans, for they think they will be heard because of their many words. Do not be like them, for your Father knows what you need before you ask him." Matthew 6:7-8 NIV

Why bother putting our petitions into words if God knows our hearts? If he already knows what we need, why do we pray for him to give it to us? Why does he provide more for one person over another? My thoughts about why prayer is necessary:

....

....

....

What if the power of prayer is not about asking and receiving, but is about getting to know God? How can my personal prayer practices bring me closer to God?

....

....

Writing my own prayers

At different times of our day or life we might pray to say thank you or to ask for guidance. We might read and reflect, spend quiet moments meditating, or ask God questions to get to know him better. We might spend prayer time just listening.

After reflecting on all the different ways I pray and the reasons I pray, my favorite form of prayer right now is:

_____

_____

_____

What would I like to change about when, where, or the way I pray?

_____

_____

_____

My personal prayer to God today is:

_____

_____

_____

_____

_____

_____

_____

Closing prayer

In the spirit of using our personal prayer time this week to grow closer to God, our friend, confidante, parent, teacher, and Lord, and with the hope of giving him a big hug one day, we close with the Prayer of St. Thomas Aquinas:

> Grant me, O Lord my God,
> a mind to know you,
> a heart to seek you,
> wisdom to find you,
> conduct pleasing to you,
> faithful perseverance in waiting for you,
> and a hope of finally embracing you.
> Amen.

Suggested topics and questions for group discussion

Use this space to prepare your own thoughts or to make notes during your group discussion.

What is your favorite form of prayer individually and as a family?

How do you receive messages from God and know God is answering?

Why do we need prayer?

_____

_____

_____

_____

When is it easier or more difficult for you to pray?

_____

_____

_____

_____

Other aspects of prayer you would like to share with others or would like to hear more about from others...

_____

_____

_____

_____

Reflection: Personal prayer practices
For your quiet reflection following group sharing.

What have I learned about myself while reflecting on and sharing thoughts about prayer practices?

_____

_____

_____

23

How have my thoughts about prayer changed?

_____

_____

_____

I was inspired by these prayer stories or ideas shared by others:

_____

_____

_____

What changes will I make in my personal prayer practices? Why?

_____

_____

_____

What prayer practices will I keep? Why?

_____

_____

_____

Resources
Resources I would like to share or that others have shared with me:

_____

_____

_____

_____

Family Traditions for
Catholic Feast Days and Holidays

Light a candle

Opening prayer

Our King

The holiday, the holy day
We await the hope you bring
Fasting, giving, prayers reflecting
The mysteries of Our King

Teaching children of your ways
Gathering with those we love
Learning that our many blessings
Come only from above

Humbly kneeling, servants all
In awesome wonder we sing
Of birth, life, death, and rising
Praise and glory to Our King!

*Ritual: any practice
or pattern of
behavior regularly
performed in a set
manner*

*Tradition: the
handing down of a
pattern of beliefs,
customs, or
practices, from
generation to
generation,
especially by word
of mouth or practice*

Family traditions

Family traditions can play an important role in helping us learn the significance of an event, remember rituals, and understand the meaning behind a celebration. Traditions can be simple or elaborate. They may involve people, gifts, readings, gatherings, food, candles, or a host of other elements. Often traditions have been passed down for several generations. Some are merged together or adapted when two families' traditions are combined. Some rituals and traditions are formed new as a person or couple reflects on the values they want to reinforce or celebrate. Even Mary and Joseph show us how important family traditions can be:

> "Given Jesus' clear knowledge and practice of the Jewish faith in his adult life, as reflected in the Gospels, it is reasonable to assume that Mary, with her husband, Joseph, practiced this Jewish religion in their home, following Torah, observing Sabbath and the festivals, reciting prayers, lighting candles, and going to synagogue, according to the custom in Galilee." —Elizabeth Johnson, C.S.J., "In Search of the Real Mary," *Catholic Update*

Consider traditions you followed as a child in your parents' home, as an adult in your own home, as part of a marriage, or in your community. How have these traditions grown? Changed? Fallen away? How did the traditions begin? What kept them going? How has your understanding of the meaning of the traditions changed over time? What makes a good tradition?

My initial thoughts about my family traditions related to Catholic feast days and holidays:

Principal feasts, holy days, and liturgical seasons

The Church's liturgical calendar begins every year on the First Sunday of Advent and runs through the Solemnity of Christ the King. Through the liturgical year, the Church celebrates the holy mysteries of Christ's birth, life, death, and resurrection. The seasons of the Church are: Advent, Christmas, Lent, Easter, and Ordinary Time. Principal feasts, holy days, and liturgical seasons include:

Advent—The liturgical season of four weeks devoted to preparation for the coming of Christ at Christmas.

Immaculate Conception (December 8)—Celebration of the belief that Mary, from the first moment of her conception in the womb of her mother, was preserved by God as immune from original sin. (Her immaculate conception in the womb of her mother, by normal sexual intercourse between her parents Sts. Joachim and Anne, should not be confused with the doctrine of the virginal conception of Mary's son Jesus.)

Christmas (December 25)—The feast of the Nativity, the birth of Jesus.

Solemnity of Mary, Mother of God (January 1)—Celebration of Mary as the mother of Jesus.

Epiphany (First Sunday following January 1)—The feast of Epiphany celebrates the revelation of Jesus as Son of God and Savior through the adoration of Jesus by the wise men (magi) from the east, his baptism in the Jordan, and the wedding feast of Cana in Galilee.

Lent—The forty-day season of fasting and prayer before Easter. The forty days represent the time Jesus spent in the desert, where he endured temptation by Satan. Lent prepares us through prayer, fasting, and giving for the death and resurrection of Jesus.

Annunciation (March 25)—Celebrates the visit of the angel Gabriel to the virgin Mary to inform her that she was to be the mother of the Savior. After giving her consent to God's word, Mary became the mother of Jesus by the power of the Holy Spirit.

Holy Week—The week preceding Easter, beginning with Palm (Passion) Sunday. It marks the Church's annual celebration of the events of Christ's passion, death, and resurrection, culminating in the Paschal Mystery.

Easter—The greatest and oldest Christian feast, which celebrates Christ's resurrection from the dead. Christians prepare for it during Lent and Holy Week, and catechumens usually receive the Sacraments of Christian Initiation (Baptism, Confirmation, Eucharist) at the Easter Vigil.

Ascension—(Thursday of the sixth week of Easter) Celebration of the bodily ascension of Jesus into heaven in the presence of his apostles, forty days following his resurrection.

Pentecost—Celebrates the descent of the Holy Spirit upon the apostles, fifty days after the resurrection of Christ (at the end of the seven weeks following Easter).

Assumption of the Blessed Virgin Mary (August 15)— Celebrates the Blessed Virgin Mary being taken up body and soul into heaven upon her death on earth.

All Saints' Day (November 1)—Commemorates all those in heaven with God. The following day, All Souls' Day, commemorates the faithful departed who have not yet been purified and reached heaven.

Solemnity of Christ the King—The last holy Sunday of the western liturgical calendar.

Family celebrations

As you review the feast days, holy days, and seasons of the church, reflect on your family's rituals and traditions for each. Then consider in more detail the preparations, activities, readings, gifts, and other elements of your rituals and traditions for the primary holiday seasons of Christmas and Easter.

Jesus is born!

"And Joseph too went up from Galilee from the town of Nazareth to Judea, to the city of David that is called Bethlehem, because he was of the house and family of David, to be enrolled with Mary, his betrothed, who was with child. While they were there, the time came for her to have her child, and she gave birth to her firstborn son. She wrapped him in swaddling clothes and laid him in a manger, because there was no room for them in the inn. Now there were shepherds in that region living in the fields and keeping the night watch over their flock. The angel of the Lord appeared to them and the glory of the Lord shone around them, and they were struck with great fear. The angel said to them, 'Do not be afraid; for behold, I proclaim to you good news of great joy that will be for all the people. For today in the city of David a savior has been born for you who is Messiah and Lord. And this will be a sign for you: you will find an infant wrapped in swaddling clothes and lying in a manger.' And suddenly there was a multitude of the heavenly host with the angel, praising God and saying: 'Glory to God in the highest and on earth peace to those on whom his favor rests.'" Luke 2:4-14 NAB

Advent and Christmas

An Advent or Christmas ritual or tradition I find particularly special or meaningful:

Ways I mark the weeks of Advent:

_____

_____

Janet decorates her tree each year with "blessings"—handmade ornaments with pictures or phrases on them. "Our many blessings include marriage, children, home, food, singing talent, good schools…"

Mary Beth sets up the nativity. Each time her child does a good deed, she puts a piece of straw in Jesus' bed. "The goal is to give him a soft bed by Christmas."

Each year, Anna bakes a homemade gift for her neighbors and her children make homemade gifts for their cousins.

The adults in Lucy's family no longer exchange gifts; instead they volunteer at a local shelter and adopt a family in need.

Charitable giving or service projects I participate in:

_____

_____

_____

My gift giving process with parents, siblings, and other adults in my family:

_____

_____

_____

How my Advent and Christmas traditions have changed from my childhood to now:

_____

_____

_____

How my siblings, parents, children, friends, neighbors, community, parish, or extended community have influenced my decisions of how I spend my time during this holiday:

_____

_____

A special Christmastime memory:

_____

_____

_____

Traditional family gatherings:

_____

_____

On Epiphany, Gail's family has a party with three gifts they each bring for Jesus: a kind deed, a new way to use a God-given talent, and a special prayer for someone in need.

Jesus is risen!

"After the sabbath, as the first day of the week was dawning, Mary Magdalene and the other Mary came to see the tomb. And behold, there was a great earthquake; for an angel of the Lord descended from heaven, approached, rolled back the stone, and sat upon it. His appearance was like lightning and his clothing was white as snow. The guards were shaken with fear of him and became like dead men. Then the angel said to the women in reply, 'Do not be afraid! I know that you are seeking Jesus the crucified. He is not here, for he has been raised just as he said. Come and see the place where he lay. Then go quickly and tell his disciples, "He has been raised from the dead, and he is going before you to Galilee; there you will see him." Behold, I have told you.' Then they went away quickly from the tomb, fearful yet overjoyed, and ran to announce this to his disciples. And behold, Jesus met them on their way and greeted them. They approached, embraced his feet, and did him homage. Then Jesus said to them, 'Do not be afraid. Go tell my brothers to go to Galilee, and there they will see me.'" Matthew 28:1-10 NAB

Lent, Holy Week, and Easter

The most powerful aspect of Lent, Holy Week, and Easter for me:

Lenten rituals that are especially meaningful to me:

In Peg's small town, teens re-enact the passion. "They carry a life-sized wooden cross. Members of the crowd walk up and using a hammer and nail, we nail to the cross pieces of paper on which we've written our sins. It's very powerful."

Ways I participate in Holy Week:

My Easter rituals and traditions:

In what ways does the Lent and Easter season change me? What do I do to bring myself closer to God at this time?

Other feast days

Other special feast days and holy days my family celebrates:

_____

_____

_____

Our special rituals and traditions for these days:

_____

_____

_____

_____

_____

Each person in Miriam's family celebrates the feast day of his or her namesake (saint) with a birthday party and a reading about the saint. "Each year, we try to find out something new about the saint's life that can serve as a guide for us in our own lives."

Ethnic heritage

Ways our ethnic heritage or other cultural traditions impact my family's holiday celebrations:

_____

_____

_____

Mixed religions

Do you have members of your family who are not Catholic? How do you honor rituals and traditions in your family?

The challenges and what we've found works for us:

_____

_____

_____

The blessings of sharing more than one religion in our family:

_____

_____

_____

_____

Commercialism/Secularism

One of the struggles of major holiday traditions is balancing the spiritual with the commercial. How does your family stay grounded in the spiritual connection while balancing commercial pressures?

Ways we have preserved the spiritual aspects of our celebrations:

_____

The children in Megan's neighborhood hunt for Easter Resurrection Eggs. Inside each egg is a Bible verse about Christ's glorious rising along with a good deed to do or a reminder of one of God's many blessings.

Ways we have combined secular and spiritual rituals:

_____

_____

_____

How did my parents help me know the difference between rituals based on religious beliefs versus those based on secular or commercial practices? How do I help my children understand the difference?

_____

_____

_____

Closing prayer

Lord, you give us so many reasons to celebrate! Help us choose the rituals and pass on the traditions that bring us closer to you; that help us better understand your life, death, and resurrection; and that teach our children the true meaning of our celebrations. Amen.

Suggested topics and questions for group discussion

Use this space to prepare your own thoughts or to make notes during your group discussion.

After reflecting on the Catholic holiday celebrations and traditions your family treasures, what are the moments most dear to you?

Show and tell. Consider bringing in a special food, game, or custom that reflects a ritual or tradition special to your family.

As we grow into our own adult lives, some traditions naturally change and evolve, others remain. How have your traditions changed? Are there changes you would like to make?

Lisa's traditions have evolved from when she was a child. "We've kept a few special rituals that have been passed through the generations. But we've also created our own. I always ask myself: 'When our kids are adults what will they be saying about the traditions they had when they were kids? Will they be meaningful enough to continue?'"

35

Why are rituals and traditions an important aspect of our faith? How does our focus on the spiritual meaning bring us closer to each other and to God?

_____

_____

_____

_____

Other aspects of Catholic holidays you would like to share with others or would like to hear more about from others...

_____

_____

_____

_____

Reflection: Family traditions for Catholic holidays
For your quiet reflection following group sharing.

What have I learned about myself while reflecting on Catholic holidays and family traditions?

_____

_____

_____

How have my thoughts about my family's traditions changed?

_____

_____

_____

I was inspired by these rituals and traditions shared by others:

_____

_____

_____

What changes will I make in how I approach special feast days and holidays ? Why?

_____

_____

_____

What aspects of my family's rituals and traditions do I want to keep? Why?

_____

_____

_____

Resources
Resources I would like to share or that others have shared with me:

_____

_____

_____

_____

_____

37

relationships

Seeing Jesus in My Relationships Changes Everything

Light a candle

Opening prayer

Lord Jesus, you loved everyone, including those who sinned, who were ill, poor, and even those who sought to do you harm. Teach me how to love my brother and sister, to care for them and to see you in every person I encounter in my day. Guide my words and actions so I may always speak and act with compassion, forgiveness, respect, and fairness. Amen.

> I have just three things to teach:
> simplicity, patience, compassion.
> These three are your greatest treasures.
> Simple in actions and in thoughts,
> you return to the source of being.
> Patient with both friends and enemies,
> you accord with the way things are.
> Compassionate towards yourself,
> you reconcile all beings in the world.
> — Lao-Tzu, *Tao Te Ching*

My relationships

The people in our lives are God's special gift to us. As you reflect on the relationships in your life, consider your parents, children, spouse, friends, business partners, coworkers, parishioners, neighbors, people you don't know in your community, political leaders, people you don't like, people who are mean to you, people you hear about in the news, people who live by values that oppose yours…all the different relationships God brings into your life no matter how briefly they stay or how dramatically or quietly they enter and leave your life.

My close relationships

The most important relationships in my life right now are:

_____

_____

_____

_____

Why are these relationships special and important to me?

_____

_____

_____

In what ways do I nurture these relationships?

_____

_____

_____

_____

How do I resolve conflicts that arise with these relationships?

A current difficult relationship
The most difficult or strained relationship in my life right now:

What circumstances make this relationship challenging?
How have I have tried to improve this relationship?

Reacting or responding: Under what circumstances would I yell at Jesus? Not share with him? Ignore him? Hold a grudge against him? Lie to him? Talk about him in a negative way? Lose patience with him? How is the way I respond to my relationship with Jesus different from the way I react to situations or respond to people in my other relationships?

Past difficult relationships
A difficult relationship from my past:

Did this resolve? What is this relationship like today? If I could change the relationship or the way we left it, what would I change?

41

What have I learned from my past difficult relationships that can help me in my relationships today?

_____

_____

_____

Relationships with acquaintances and strangers
A time I felt God brought someone into my life for a short time:

_____

_____

_____

What did I learn from this person? How did I respond to this relationship?

_____

_____

_____

Jesus teaches us how to love
Jesus teaches us through his example how to have loving relationships. As we see Jesus in our relationships we come to an awareness of the relationship he wants to have with us and the relationships he wants us to have with others. Among the many ways Jesus teaches us to nurture our relationships and resolve conflicts, he teaches us to have compassion, to listen, to forgive, to be kind, and to love others as he loves us.

Compassion

> "Seeing the people, He felt compassion for them, because they were distressed and dispirited like sheep without a shepherd." Matthew 9:36 NASB

"Moved with compassion, Jesus touched their eyes; and immediately they regained their sight and followed Him."
Matthew 20:34 NASB

"And the king will say to them in reply, 'Amen, I say to you, whatever you did for one of these least brothers of mine, you did for me." Matthew 25:40 NAB

Compassion is the awareness of another person's distress along with a desire to alleviate it. We might not be able to heal all around us who suffer, but we can each help at least one other person. We can offer a compassionate and listening heart, cook a meal, share a portion of our wealth, give our time and talent to help someone get through a tough time.

What suffering do I see in the people around me that I could help alleviate?

_____

_____

_____

If I could set down my load for a day and carry someone else's, whose burden would I choose to carry?

_____

_____

_____

"Then Jesus said, 'He who has ears to hear, let him hear.'"
Mark 4:9 NIV

Jesus taught us to listen with our ears and also with our hearts. He taught us to listen to his word and then put it into action. Listening is the first step. As we go about our busy stressful days, do we take time to listen to others? Or do we wait for our turn to talk?

43

When I need a good listener, what qualities am I looking for?

_____

_____

_____

Am I a good listener? Can I listen without speaking my own mind? Without trying to fix a situation? What has listening taught me?

_____

_____

_____

How does listening to others help me do God's work?

_____

_____

_____

Forgiveness

> "Then Peter approaching asked him, 'Lord, if my brother sins against me, how often must I forgive him? As many as seven times?' Jesus answered, 'I say to you, not seven times but seventy-seven times.'" Matthew 18:21-22 NAB

> "When you stand to pray, forgive anyone against whom you have a grievance, so that your heavenly Father may in turn forgive you your transgressions." Mark 11:25-26 NAB

> "For this is my blood of the covenant, which will be shed on behalf of many for the forgiveness of sins." Matthew 26:28 NAB

Forgiveness is a matter of the heart. Forgiving someone requires that we no longer feel any resentment toward them. There is no debt to repay. No further apologies to accept. All injuries are forgotten. Both the person giving and receiving forgiveness receive grace. We may find it difficult to forgive someone who has hurt us, especially if that person has never apologized. But forgiving them is our act and requires our change of heart, not theirs. If they repeat their offense, still we can forgive. We cannot control someone else's hurtful acts, but we can control our response to them. We can forgive them seventy-seven times.

A time when I found it difficult to forgive someone:

_____

_____

_____

A time I might have hurt someone and not apologized:

_____

_____

_____

Ways I have reconciled differences with others in the past:

_____

_____

_____

If I were able to immediately forgive and forget, how might it change my relationships?

_____

_____

It can be paralyzing to brood over past events or relationships even though we know we cannot undo what has been done. When do we need to reconcile the past? When is it okay to simply move forward?

"Therefore, laying aside falsehood, speak truth each one of you with his neighbor, for we are members of one another. Be angry, and yet do not sin; do not let the sun go down on your anger, and do not give the devil an opportunity." Ephesians 4:25-27 NASB

Do I go to bed angry? How do I resolve anger in a timely manner and yet wait long enough to get perspective?

_____

_____

_____

"But I tell you: Love your enemies and pray for those who persecute you, that you may be sons of your Father in heaven. He causes his sun to rise on the evil and the good, and sends rain on the righteous and the unrighteous. If you love those who love you, what reward will you get?…And if you greet only your brothers, what are you doing more than others?" Matthew 5: 44-47 NIV

It is especially difficult to reconcile difficult relationships if we don't like the person or if we have no desire to continue the relationship. Relationships take time and work. Take a moment to consider a failed relationship. Could it be you misunderstood that person's perspective? If you now look at that person as Jesus, do you see them any differently? If you were forced to continue to interact with that person in your daily life now, how would you work it out?

Reflecting on a past difficult relationship with a compassionate and forgiving heart, how could I mend this relationship?

_____

_____

I expect God to forgive me when I hurt him. Have I ever felt hurt by God? How did we reconcile?

Love and kindness

"As I have loved you, so you must love one another." John 13:34 NIV

Jesus loved us enough to die for us. How much love can we pass around in a day? Love is infinite. We will never run out. We can always make more. So what stops us from giving away as much love as we can each day? A smile. A hug. An open heart. A listening ear. A kind deed. A handwritten love letter. A call to an old friend. A game with a child. An image of hope for someone who is hurting. There are so many ways we can stop for a moment and share our love.

An act of love someone shared with me that has stuck with me:

A person I can think of right now who might need my love:

What kind word or deed did I share with my family or a friend today?

47

When do I find myself not being kind to the people who are closest to me—my parents, siblings, spouse, children, or good friends?

How does my own self-esteem and love for myself affect how I participate in a relationship? Do I see myself as Jesus sees me?

Three new ways I can share my love this week:

Relationship environments

In our daily lives, there are certain environments in which we regularly build relationships: at home, at work, at church, in our community. Consider the environments in which you regularly build relationships. Do you treat people in one environment with more or less respect or patience or humility than other people in your life? How do environmental factors such as decision-making authority, stress, positive and negative attitudes, routines, fresh air, lighting, cleanliness, welcoming opportunities, and perceived or real hierarchies affect your ability to nurture relationships in these environments? In what ways can you create a place within each environment to invite Jesus?

At home

How does my current home environment positively or negatively affect my relationships?

_____

_____

_____

Does my family consider our home a sacred place? Do we think of God being there with us at our meals, in our intimate conversations? How does setting a place for Jesus at our table change our dinner conversation?

_____

_____

_____

What are some ways I can bring Jesus into our home and our daily routines?

_____

_____

_____

If Jesus and I had to work out our family roles—who would do the laundry, run the business, clean the bathroom, pick up the kids, and so on—how would I approach the situation differently than I do now with my family?

_____

_____

_____

_____

If it were Jesus I was helping to get ready for school or work in the morning or interacting with at other key times of our daily routine, how would I approach those transition times differently?

If Jesus were living in my home, what changes would I make to our environment to accommodate him?

At work
How does my current work environment positively or negatively affect my relationships?

Sometimes decisions at work or with a coworker affect our lives and jobs in significant ways (e.g., maternity leave, layoffs, salaries, responsibilities). When did an important decision at work affect my own or a coworker's livelihood? Was Jesus involved in that decision?

How does seeing Jesus in my coworkers change the way I approach situations at work?

_____

_____

_____

_____

At church
What types of relationships do I have with people at my church? What opportunities does my church provide for me to build and nurture relationships?

_____

_____

_____

_____

Does this environment of a group of people who all love Jesus make it easier for me to begin and nurture good relationships?

_____

_____

_____

_____

In my community and world
Ways my neighbors help me see Jesus in others:

_____

_____

_____

Does thinking of a stranger as Jesus change my desire to know the person? Concerns or worries I have about building relationships in my community:

Times when it's difficult for me to see Jesus in my neighborhood and community:

When I think of those less fortunate, how does thinking of them as Jesus change my desire to help them?

Bringing it all together

After reflecting on my relationships; considering what Jesus teaches me about compassion, forgiveness, and love; and thinking about ways my home, work, and community environments support or strain my relationships, how can I use what I've learned to nurture my relationships with others as I would with Jesus?

Closing prayer

Lord, you give me the blessing of relationships—both challenging and rewarding—with my family, friends, coworkers, strangers, community, and greater world. Help me see your face in each and every person I meet. Be with me in my conversations, brief encounters, and lifelong friendships. Use me to bring your grace to those who need it. Grant me the strength and wisdom to use my listening heart, kindness, compassion, forgiveness, patience, and love in every situation. Gently remind me to treat each relationship you bring into my life with the same care in which I nurture my relationship with you, for you are in every person. Thank you for this gift. Amen.

Suggested topics and questions for group discussion

Use this space to prepare your own thoughts or to make notes during your group discussion.

When conflicts arise in your relationships, how do you resolve them? What makes it easy or difficult for you to forgive others?

In what ways do you show love and compassion to others? How do you respond differently to your close relationships than to strangers?

How does your environment at home, work, church, or in your community affect your relationships?

_____

_____

_____

_____

How does thinking about seeing Jesus in your relationships change the way you view your relationships?

_____

_____

_____

_____

Other aspects of relationships you would like to share with others or would like to hear more about from others...

_____

_____

_____

_____

Reflection: Seeing Jesus in my relationships

For your quiet reflection following group sharing.

What have I learned about myself after reflecting on my important relationships and thinking of Jesus in those relationships?

_____

_____

_____

How have my thoughts about my relationships changed?

_____

_____

How can my relationships be improved or nurtured differently if I treat those people as I would treat Jesus?

_____

_____

I was inspired by these stories or ideas shared by others:

_____

_____

What changes will I make in the way I resolve conflict or nurture relationships? Why?

_____

_____

What will I continue to do when resolving conflict or nurturing relationships? Why?

_____

_____

Resources

Resources I would like to share or that others have shared with me:

_____

_____

_____

_____

_____

_____

Mary, Mother of Jesus;
Mother Teresa;
My Personal Role Model

Light a candle

Opening prayer

Hail, Mary. Full of grace, the Lord is with thee. Blessed art thou among women and blessed is the fruit of thy womb, Jesus. Holy Mary, Mother of God. Pray for us sinners, now and at the hour of our death. Amen.

Mary, Mother of Jesus

Imagine being the mother of Jesus. The great joy of giving birth to God's son, the knowledge that your child would bring the greatest gift to the world. The deep sorrow at your child's suffering and death. While we don't have a lot of details to tell us about the life of Mary, what we do know tells us enough about her love of and obedience to God to make her an amazing spiritual role model.

Blessed is she who believed

"The Virgin Mary most perfectly embodies the obedience of faith. By faith Mary welcomes the tidings and promise brought by the angel Gabriel, believing that 'with God nothing will be impossible' (Luke 1:37) and so giving her assent: 'Behold I am the handmaid of the Lord; let it be [done] to me according to your word.' (Luke 1:38) Elizabeth greeted her: 'Blessed is she who believed that there would be a fulfillment of what was spoken to her from the Lord.' (Luke 1:45) It is for this faith that all generations have called Mary blessed. Throughout her life and until her last ordeal when Jesus her son died on the cross, Mary's faith never wavered. She never ceased to believe in the fulfillment of God's word. And so the Church venerates in Mary the purest realization of faith." *Catechism of the Catholic Church* (148-149)

Mary's faith was unwavering her whole life, no matter what the trial. She completely and freely said yes to what God asked her to do, even becoming pregnant as a virgin. How scary that must have been—who would believe her? Yet she completely trusted God.

Do I completely trust God? When do I have the most difficulty trusting?

Mary's life managing the household

In her daily life as a first century Jewish woman, Mary worked hard to care for and nurture her family in their home in the rural village of Nazareth. Her neighbors were peasants and craftsmen. Like the village women of her day, Mary was probably illiterate. Her husband, Joseph, was the local carpenter. She may have had several children living in her home to care for—Joseph's children from a previous marriage or Jesus' first cousins, often called brothers and sisters in those days ("Is he not the carpenter, the son of Mary, and the brother of James and Joses and Judas and Simon? Are not his sisters here with us?" Mark 6:3 NAB). Nazareth was part of an occupied state under imperial Rome, marked by violence and poverty. It was a tough life by any standard.

As a hardworking wife and mother managing her household during tough political and economic times, Mary is a woman who understands the demands we face every day.

Do I complain about the work I do to manage my home and care for my family or do I do it joyfully? How can I find more joy in it?

How can I look to Mary for encouragement in my daily tasks? How does this image of Mary help me see my role as a homemaker— aside from any other role I have—as one of service to God?

Mary's trust as a mother

"And when he was twelve years old, they went up according to the festival custom. After they had completed its days, as they were returning, the boy Jesus remained behind in Jerusalem, but his parents did not know it. Thinking that he was in the caravan, they journeyed for a day and looked for him among their relatives and acquaintances, but not finding him, they returned to Jerusalem to look for him. After three days they found him in the temple, sitting in the midst of the teachers, listening to them and asking them questions, and all who heard him were astounded at his understanding and his answers. When his parents saw him, they were astonished, and his mother said to him, 'Son, why have you

59

done this to us? Your father and I have been looking for you with great anxiety.' And he said to them, 'Why were you were looking for me? Did you not know that I must be in my Father's house?' But they did not understand what he said to them. He went down with them and came to Nazareth, and was obedient to them; and his mother kept all these things in her heart. And Jesus advanced (in) wisdom and age and favor before God and man." Luke 2:42-52 NAB

Today, many parents feel they must know a child's whereabouts every moment of the day. So at first it might be hard to understand how his parents didn't notice that Jesus stayed behind. It was common in that time for extended families to live near each other and to travel together. The men likely traveled alongside the other men, the women with other women and young children. The older children, such as Jesus, probably traveled in a group together. The children were cared for by the larger extended family. So it's not surprising that Mary did not know where Jesus was each moment. Still, when she did discover his absence and began looking for him, she must have ached with the same worry we feel in moments when we've "lost" a child.

Times I worry most about my children:

What are some ways I can put my worries to rest?

When Mary hears what Jesus says about being in the temple, she treasures it in her heart. When has my child shown wisdom and a sense of his own mission?

_____

_____

_____

My hopes for my children:

_____

_____

_____

Mary's suffering

Mary watched her son be crucified even though he did not commit a crime. She saw the soldiers casting lots for his clothes. She watched her child suffer and die. Yet she remained faithful to God. She continued her service to God even after the worst a mother can imagine had taken place.

> "Then the soldiers, when they had crucified Jesus, took His outer garments and made four parts, a part to every soldier and also the tunic; now the tunic was seamless, woven in one piece. So they said to one another, 'Let us not tear it, but cast lots for it, to decide whose it shall be'; this was to fulfill the Scripture: 'they divided my outer garments among them, and for my clothing they cast lots.' Therefore the soldiers did these things. But standing by the cross of Jesus were His mother, and His mother's sister, Mary the wife of Clopas, and Mary Magdalene. When Jesus then saw His mother, and the disciple whom He loved standing nearby, He said to His mother, 'Woman, behold, your son!' Then He said to the disciple, 'Behold, your mother!' From that hour the disciple took her into his own household." John 19: 23-27 NASB

How can Mary's faith help me with my own losses? What losses have occurred in my life that I could look to Mary for help?

_____

_____

_____

Even in his last moments, Jesus looked out for his mother, ensuring she would be taken care of after his death. Jesus also puts loved ones in my life. How do my loved ones ensure I am cared for?

_____

_____

Mary's courage

Mary is often thought of as meek and obedient, but she was also courageous. She combined humility with strength. She raised children, lived a poor and hardworking life, witnessed her son's brutal death—and faced it all with courage and faith.

In what ways do I show that strength in my everyday life?

_____

_____

_____

Mary, a faithful leader among men

"When they had entered the city, they went up to the upper room where they were staying; that is, Peter and John and James and Andrew, Philip and Thomas, Bartholomew and Matthew, James the son of Alphaeus, and Simon the Zealot, and Judas the son of James. These all with one mind were continually devoting themselves to prayer, along with the women, and Mary the mother of Jesus, and with His brothers." Acts 1: 13-14 NASB

Mary continued to pray faithfully and to participate with Jesus' disciples in what were the beginnings of the Christian faith. How does her example help me keep going with my own faith journey even after painful events in my life?

_____

_____

_____

What about Mary's steadfast leadership qualities can we apply to today's boardroom and other gatherings?

_____

_____

_____

Mary's humbleness

"And Mary said, 'My soul proclaims the greatness of the Lord; my spirit rejoices in God my savior. For he has looked upon his handmaid's lowliness; behold, from now on will all ages call me blessed. The Mighty One has done great things for me, and holy is his name.'" Luke 1: 46-49 NAB

Mary knows that God has blessed her. She is in awe of the fact that because of what God has asked her to do, all ages will call her blessed. Her task is not only life-changing for her but for all generations to come.

Reflecting on something I have done really well, do I feel humbled, as Mary did, that God chose me? Do I believe that my gift, my ability, my success is due to God?

_____

_____

_____

In what ways will the results of my service to God have a lasting effect on others?

_____

_____

_____

Praying to Mary

"With Elizabeth we marvel, 'And why is this granted me, that the mother of my Lord should come to me?' Because she gives us Jesus, her son, Mary is Mother of God and our mother; we can entrust all our cares and petitions to her... By entrusting ourselves to her prayer, we abandon ourselves to the will of God together with her: 'Thy will be done.' ... By asking Mary to pray for us, we acknowledge ourselves to be poor sinners... We give ourselves over to her now, in the Today of our lives. And our trust broadens further...to surrender 'the hour of our death' wholly to her care. May she be there as she was at her son's death on the cross. May she welcome us as our mother at the hour of our passing to lead us to her son, Jesus, in paradise." *Catechism of the Catholic Church* (2677)

Mary, Mother of Jesus, you endured both joy and heartache raising your son, our Lord, Jesus. Teach us to have your patience as we raise our children. Help us trust fully in God just as you put your whole life in his service. You know the pain of a loved one dying. Comfort us in our times of sorrow. You lived your life free of sin. Be our guide as we make our choices. Grant us your humbleness and daily courage. Teach us to be steadfast, loyal, and faithful leaders.

My special prayer to Mary:

_____

_____

_____

Mother Teresa

Mother Teresa, born Agnes Gonxha Bojaxhiu in Albania in 1910, was a Roman Catholic nun. While traveling to the Loreto convent in 1946 for her annual retreat, she had a calling to leave the convent and help the poor while living among them. She began her missionary work with the poor in 1948. Teresa wrote in her diary that in her first year she had no income and had to resort to begging for food and supplies. Teresa experienced doubt, loneliness, and the temptation to return to the comfort of convent life. She wrote:

> "Our Lord wants me to be a free nun covered with the
> poverty of the cross. Today I learned a good lesson. The
> poverty of the poor must be so hard for them. While looking
> for a home I walked and walked till my arms and legs ached.
> I thought how much they must ache in body and soul,
> looking for a home, food and health. Then the comfort of
> Loreto came to tempt me. 'You have only to say the word
> and all that will be yours again,' the Tempter kept on saying...
> Of free choice, my God, and out of love for you, I desire to
> remain and do whatever be your Holy will in my regard."
> —Mother Teresa (quoted in *Mother Teresa: A Complete
> Authorized Biography* by Kathryn Spink)

Teresa received Vatican permission in 1950 to start the Missionaries of Charity. Its mission was to care for, in her own words, "the hungry, the naked, the homeless, the crippled, the blind, the lepers, all those people who feel unwanted, unloved, uncared for throughout society, people that have become a burden to the society and are shunned by everyone." It began as a small order with 13 members in Calcutta and grew to more than 4,000 nuns running orphanages, AIDS hospices, and charity centers worldwide, and caring for refugees, the blind, disabled, aged, alcoholics, the poor and homeless, and victims of floods, epidemics, and famine. In 1979, Mother Teresa was awarded the Nobel Peace Prize, "for work undertaken in the struggle to overcome poverty and distress, which also constitute a threat to peace." She refused the conventional ceremonial banquet and asked

65

that the money instead be given to the poor in India, stating that earthly rewards were important only if they helped her help the world's needy. When Mother Teresa received the prize, she was asked, "What can we do to promote world peace?" She answered, "Go home and love your family." Mother Teresa died in 1997. After her death she was beatified by Pope John Paul II and given the title Blessed Teresa of Calcutta.

Mother Teresa did extraordinary things in her lifetime. Having her as a spiritual role model does not mean we have the same calling, yet we can look to her example for spiritual guidance in many ways.

Personal sacrifice and perseverance
Mother Teresa gave up a lot to answer God's call for her. At age 18, she left her home to train as a nun. To understand and truly help the poor, she lived in poverty herself, among the poor, sick, and homeless in India's slums.

What would I be willing to give up if I were asked?

What are some ways I can better understand the needs of those less fortunate in my own community—those with less education, fewer job options, financial difficulties, serious illnesses?

Mother Teresa listened to God's call even when she had nothing and was tempted to return to her convent, where she could find the worldly comforts she needed.

When have I been tempted to give up? What keeps me going?

_____

_____

_____

Mother Teresa asked that the money traditionally spent on the Nobel Peace Prize banquet be instead used to feed the poor. What are some ways I can forgo receiving praise, credit, or gifts for work I have done?

_____

_____

_____

What are some examples of waste in our community where resources spent on nice but unnecessary luxuries could be spent improving others' lives?

_____

_____

_____

Great love

"We should not ask to do great things for God but to do small things with great love." —Mother Teresa

How can everything I do today be done with great love? What reminders can I put in place to help me make each act my best and most loving?

_____

_____

_____

In my own community, what are some ways I could make a significant, lasting difference in at least one other person's life?

A crisis of faith

After Mother Teresa's death, several of her letters, written over decades of her work with the poor and collected in support of a petition for her sainthood, revealed her struggle to find God present in her life and work.

> "Jesus has a very special love for you. As for me, the silence and the emptiness is so great, that I look and do not see,— Listen and do not hear—the tongue moves [in prayer] but does not speak ... I want you to pray for me—that I let him have free hand." —Mother Teresa to the Rev. Michael Van Der Peet, September 1979

Despite the silence she experienced and her feeling that Jesus was not there, Mother Teresa found ways to maintain her faith and her good works. Is there a time I questioned the presence of God? What allowed me to continue on my path? To find God again?

Mary and Mother Teresa both heard God's call and followed, even in their darkest times. How can I keep God's calling for me strong and focused in my life?

Am I ready to say yes to whatever God asks me to do?

_____

_____

How does using Mary and Mother Teresa as spiritual role models
help me on my spiritual path?

_____

_____

Personal spiritual role model
What type of people do I believe make good spiritual role models?

_____

_____

Women who inspire me the most tend to have these qualities:

_____

_____

Who in my life has been a special example of Christ's love? How did
this person come into my life?

_____

_____

_____

What changes have I made in my life because of this person?

_____

_____

_____

69

Am I a role model? What can I do to become a good spiritual role model for someone else?

Closing prayer

Mary, Mother of God, watch over me. You inspire me with your complete trust in God and unwavering faith, even when God asked you to do what seemed impossible, even when you faced great suffering. Help me love and care for my family and humbly and courageously serve our Lord as you did.

Oh God, you call me to serve you just as you called Mary and Mother Teresa to serve you. I know that I, too, may have to endure hardships and suffering just as they did in doing your will. Give me the courage to say "Yes" to whatever you ask. Mother Teresa continued her work even when she couldn't hear you answer her prayers. Send me comfort and encouragement to continue on my path even when the way is hard and I feel alone. I know you are with me always. I will look to the role models you give me in my life to remind me of your love. Amen.

Suggested topics and questions for group discussion

Use this space to prepare your own thoughts or to make notes during your group discussion.

What about Mary's character most resonates with you?

In what ways does Mother Teresa's struggle and accomplishment inspire you?

_____

_____

_____

_____

Who is someone who has been a role model for you and how has that person influenced your life?

_____

_____

_____

_____

Other aspects of spiritual role models you would like to share with others or would like to hear more about from others...

_____

_____

_____

Reflection: Spiritual role models
For your quiet reflection following group sharing.

What struck me most about the lives and faith of Mary and Mother Teresa?

_____

_____

_____

71

What have I learned about myself while reflecting on and sharing thoughts about Mary, Mother Teresa, and my own personal spiritual role models?

_____

_____

_____

_____

I was inspired by these stories or ideas shared by others:

_____

_____

_____

_____

How will I use the lessons from my spiritual role models to help guide me in my daily life?

_____

_____

_____

_____

Resources
Resources I would like to share or that others have shared with me:

_____

_____

_____

_____

Money & Wealth

Light a candle

Opening prayer

> *Wealth*
> The sun rises at His command
> Wind caresses the trees
> whose leaves turn and bend and fall
> and grow anew with the seasons
> The ocean embraces and holds the earth
> yet knows its limits
>
> Mountains rise in praise and glory
> Stars glimmer on the edge of eternity
> reminders of life yet to come
> windows for angels watching over us
>
> These, God's possessions
> Gifts of Beauty, Power, Love
> His Wealth shared freely

CIRCLE OF
CATHOLIC WOMEN
journal one

steward

broader

striving

Lord, give me only what I need and help me to be satisfied. Guide me in my desires and decisions about wealth and possessions. Help me to be a good steward of the many gifts you entrust to me and my family. Thank you for your generosity. Please help me to be generous and freely share my gifts with others knowing that all things come from you. Amen.

As you reflect on your values and beliefs toward money and wealth, consider all the many ways God blesses you and your family. Wealth is much broader than a bank account. In what ways do you consider yourself wealthy? In what ways has your wealth changed over the years? How have decisions about money affected your relationships, your standard of living, your choices in other areas of your life? Has your view of money and wealth helped bring you closer to God?

As I begin this chapter, these are my thoughts about money and wealth:

- About money : My husband made almost 100k per year what seems a fortune, but we spend it all and even more. Our credit cards are high and our savings none.
- Wealth - Some people may think we are wealthy, because we own a brand new, colonial house, and we got a brand new car, and have one of my

These are questions I have about money and wealth in my life: kids in private school, but

How to live in a budget? (written) I don't feel that way

is it wealth refer just to money possessions I cannot travel to see my family back in Peru

or it can be ~~talent~~ related to talents? and have no idea when we will be able to.

On being rich

"It's much better to be wise and sensible than to be rich."
Proverbs 16:16 CEV

"It is easier for a camel to pass through the eye of a needle than for one who is rich to enter the kingdom of God." Mark 10:25 NAB

"People who want to get rich fall into temptation and a trap and into many foolish and harmful desires that plunge men into ruin and destruction. For the love of money is a root of all kinds of evil. <u>Some people, eager for money, have</u> <u>wandered from the faith and pierced themselves with many</u> <u>griefs."</u> 1 Timothy 6:9-10 NIV

What is my definition of a <u>rich pers</u>on?

> So me one with a lot posessing
> able to take vacation . and
> have their kids in private schools .
> Able to buy things as he/she please .

Am I rich? Am I poor? Somewhere in between?

> Somewhere in between.
> - own a house /2 cars / kids in different activities
> with time too clothe /shoe
> but not Vacation / shopping / not dining
> out .

We work hard to gather enough money to provide a good living for our families, to <u>manage</u> debts, to live comfortably. Is there anything wrong with ⟨striving⟩ for more money?

> I think if we are too worry about
> it, this can keep you awake at nights.
> Also if you decide to work more hours, that
> is time that you could use with your family

Joann lives paycheck to paycheck. "I live within my budget and try to save, but it's hard when unexpected expenses come up, with my car or computer, for example."

Helen worries about her retirement. "How do I know how much I need in case I get sick versus sharing it now with my children or a charity?"

Kyla saves half of every pay raise to help improve her standard of living and save for the future or for unforeseen challenges. She gives the other half to charity in thanksgiving.

"Keep falsehood and lies far from me; give me neither poverty nor riches, but give me only my daily bread. Otherwise, I may have too much and disown you and say, 'Who is the Lord?' Or I may become poor and steal, and so dishonor the name of my God." Proverbs 30:8-9 NIV

How do I make decisions for myself or with my family about how much money we need? How do I know when we have enough?

My husban and I have a budget we know that our expenses are at equal as much as he income and that we will need few years to be debt free. We need another income but I have to stay at home and take care of my kids. So, we need to reduce our expenses.

Choices & intent

"You cannot be the slave of two masters! You will like one more than the other or be more loyal to one than the other. You cannot serve both God and money." Matthew 6:24 CEV

"But more than anything else, put God's work first and do what he wants. Then the other things will be yours as well." Matthew 6:33 CEV

One of the challenges of adulthood and forming our own family is making decisions about balancing work and money and family time. Many factors influence our decisions about how much we need and want to work and what kind of work we take on, including the cost of living in our community, available jobs, educational opportunities, childcare costs, health insurance needs, and our desire to spend more time with our family. Married couples make decisions about one partner working fewer hours or staying home to care for children. We make decisions about public, private, and homeschool education for our children. How many cars we park in our garage. How many bedrooms and bathrooms in our home. Which neighborhood to live in. Whether to move to a new location for a different opportunity. How close or far away we live from extended family. Each of our decisions involves a combination of financial needs and values. For each, there is a sacrifice of time or money.

My current choices regarding jobs, family time, and living costs:

Jobs : Ed works and I stay at home

family time : we spend weekends together (Is it possible to work just few hours on Weekend)

living costs : very high.

What values or changes in my life prompted these decisions?

Jobs : we think kids need the love of their mother when they are littles.

Family time : we believe it is important to share good times

living - costs : We were expecting a second child, had my sister with us and we thought we needed a bigger house

Is everyone in my family happy with these choices? What sacrifices do we make to attain money? What sacrifices would I like to trade?

My kids love to have a big house, however my husband and I have asked ourselve if we should move to a smaller place with smaller mortgage - sacrifices, we have not be able to visit my family in Peru since 2012.

Are we struggling financially? Is this due to factors within or outside our control? How has this affected my daily choices?

Yes! I think my husband and I can not live within a budget, he likes new technology, brand clothing, brand cars, And I want to have my kids in different activities like swimming + ball, gym and spent more than I should. I think this is within our control. Not much, my husband buy what he likes.

My neighbors' wealth

"Do not want anything that belongs to someone else. Don't want anyone's house, wife or husband, slaves, oxen, donkeys or anything else." Exodus 20:17 CEV

Jasmyn's husband works long hours and often travels away from home. "We don't always agree on the sacrifices. I feel he should be home with us more and he's trying to do his best to keep a good career and support our family. The choices aren't always easy."

When I reflect on purchases my family and I have made, decisions about where to live, cars we drive, and so on, are there any I feel we've made because of what others were doing?

Not really, I think Ed and I are dreamers. And we do have c/c that make us believe we can afford what we want.

Good stewards
God calls us to be good stewards of what we receive.

> "You should take good care of your sheep and goats."
> Proverbs 27:23 CEV

In what ways do I take good care of the financial gifts God entrusts to me and my family?

I think I do not take good care of the financial gifts God entrusts to me.

Charity and sacrifice
God also calls us to share.

> "All the believers were one in heart and mind. No one claimed that any of his possessions was his own, but they shared everything they had. There were no needy persons among them. For from time to time those who owned lands or houses sold them, brought the money from the sales and put it at the apostles' feet, and it was distributed to anyone as he had need." Acts 4:32, 34-35 NIV

> "What good is it, my brothers, if a man claims to have faith but has no deeds? Can such faith save him? Suppose a brother or sister is without clothes and daily food. If one of you says to him, 'Go, I wish you well; keep warm and well fed,'

but does nothing about his physical needs, what good is it?
In the same way, faith by itself, if it is not accompanied by
action, is dead." James 2:14-17 NIV

values & beliefs
MONEY & WEALTH

How can I be of help?

"Be generous, and someday you will be rewarded."
Ecclesiastes 11:1 CEV

What choices have I made about sharing the possessions and
wealth God has entrusted to me to care for? Do I have difficulty
giving up what feels like "mine"? Do I think of these as God's gifts to
be shared and my responsibility to make sure others have some?

*My husband and I ~~shared~~ hosted my youngest
sister for about 3 years, we share with her our
house and paid for her ESL classes. We share what we had and even more.
(I mean we had to use c/c to pay for her last year of school)*

"A poor widow came and put in two very small copper coins,
worth only a fraction of a penny. Calling his disciples to him,
Jesus said, 'I tell you the truth, this poor widow has put more
into the treasury than all the others. They all gave out of
their wealth; but she, out of her poverty, put in everything—
all she had to live on.'" Mark 12:42-44 NIV

How often do we give away food we don't like, clothes we no
longer wear, appliances or toys that are worn out? How often
do we give away something difficult to part with? What if for
Christmas we gave toys our children wanted to the poor and
not to our own children? What if instead of buying ourselves
a new shirt, we wore the old one and gave the new one
away? What sacrifices do we make in our giving?

My giving philosophy:

*~~Give~~ Help your family and friends, but never
go above your limits! I mean do not ~~use a c/c~~ get a loan
to donate to "charity" ~~or even to~~ or to try to help
a friend or relative. Instead try to give him/her an advise
that he/she can use it.*

*When Tara's apartment
building burned to the
ground all she had left
was the bag of clothes
she had put in her car
that morning to give to
Goodwill. "I learned
what it was like to
receive my own
giveaway items."*

79

What gift of money, time, talent, or possession would be a sacrifice for me that would help someone else? What stops me from giving it away freely?

I could donate some money to my local parish, but I feel lik I should pay my debts first. I could go back to the way, but at the end of the day a I am so tired to go.

Do I feel I "deserve" the money and possessions I own? Are there times I feel someone else deserves them less than I do?

My husband work hard to provide for his famaly and I do, my best to take care of my kids, my husband and the house.

"Whoever loves money never has money enough; whoever loves wealth is never satisfied with his income. ... The sleep of a laborer is sweet, whether he eats little or much, but the abundance of a rich man permits him no sleep. Naked a man comes from his mother's womb, and as he comes, so he departs. He takes nothing from his labor that he can carry in his hand." Ecclesiastes 5:10, 12, 15 NIV

"'One thing you lack,' he said. 'Go, sell everything you have and give to the poor, and you will have treasure in heaven. Then come, follow me.'" Mark 10:21 NIV

"Command those who are rich in this present world not to be arrogant nor to put their hope in wealth, which is so uncertain, but to put their hope in God, who richly provides us with everything for our enjoyment. Command them to do good, to be rich in good deeds, and to be generous and willing to share. In this way they will lay up treasure for themselves as a firm foundation for the coming age, so that they may take hold of the life that is truly life." 1 Timothy 6:17-19 NIV

How do I determine my giving plan to my church, to the poor, and to other charities?

- We do give some money to the church on the Mass.
- We donate kids baby/kids gear /clothes in good conditions
- we donate to some charities for thanksgiving / christmas

How do I choose the organizations and causes I support?

try to find those who give the
most to their cause.

to the poor

Chris strives to live as simply as possible. "I am so blessed—with a home, freedoms, loving relationships. I have much to share with others."

What happens when our income or financial situation changes? How does it affect our giving plan?

Few years ago, we used to send money to my mom to help her cover her expenses, when we brought my sister here, We stopped that because we had an extra mouth to feed, then we she went back, we just stop helping them ..

"If we would measure fully the blessing of simplicity we must look beyond this world. We must try to imagine… what it will be some day… to bring our life, our character, bare and unsheltered into His Presence."
—Rev. Francis Paget, 1898

How do I share my best self, my enthusiasm, trust, talents, presence, and other non-monetary aspects of my wealth with others?

We are trying to balance our finance

I try to be friendly and smile to people who seems to be friendly to me or my kids. I have a WBs group who with I share my faith and believe. Try to be positive and look for God'.

Lessons we learn
Wealth comes in many sizes. Ten dollars is a fortune to a young child. As we age, we develop different perspectives of money. As we accumulate wealth, we learn more about how to invest money, budget for it, work for it, spend it, waste it, and so on. We express both our need for and value of money by the choices we make—the

hours spent at a job instead of with family, volunteer jobs we are
willing to do without pay to further a cause. Each of our values gets
communicated to others around us through our decisions and
actions.

What lessons do I consciously teach my children about money?

When they ask for a toy, I say
"I have no money"; or explain that we do
have money for other purposes than toys.

What other lessons am I teaching my children through my choices
and actions?

I teach them to ~~see~~ be carefull
how do they use the electricaly and water.
"tearn off the lights when you leave a room, do not waste

What beliefs about money does my spouse demonstrate? water when
washing your
hands.
It is ok to have a balance in
one or 2 c/c

What have I learned from my parents, extended family, friends,
neighbors, or parishioners about money through their choices?

My mom lived ~~with they~~ in a tight
budget, she did buy cloth for her kids
twice a year and do not dine out.

What worries me most about money in the short-term? Long-term?

Debt /

I wish I could travel to Peru
to see my family, but I can not
until we pay the c/c.

An aspect of money and wealth in my life I feel really good about:

· I do share what I have with my relatives in Peru. I helped my mom for a couple of year, then brought my sister, and allways send something for my other youy brothers.

An aspect of money and wealth in my life I'm uncomfortable with:

Debts.

Other ways I feel wealthy that have nothing to do with money:

· I do have a husband and 3 beautiful kids
· I do have family and friend that care about us
· I do have Jesus in my life .

Closing prayer

She awoke in the morning with bills to pay and errands to run and jobs to do. But first, she prayed: "Thank you Lord for all you have given me. Help me to be a good and kind person and to do your will." Then she went to her husband and children and loved them and gave them all they needed. She helped a neighbor and gave hope to a stranger. When they tried to repay her, she smiled and said, "God bless you." At the end of the day, she had finished God's work first and he blessed her. She prayed: "Thank you Lord for all you have given me."

Lord, let me put your work first in my day. Let me love my family, my neighbor, and the strangers you put before me. I will give without expecting reward or credit, especially when it requires great sacrifice. I know that when I put your work first in my day, all else will come as I need. And that will be enough. Amen.

Suggested topics and questions for group discussion
Use this space to prepare your own thoughts or to make notes during your group discussion.

What is your definition of rich?

- A person with a good financial position.

- A person with talent.

The choices we make about our wealth aren't always easy. Are you happy with your choices? What would you like to change?

Not completely. I wonder if moving to
a smaller house and have my oldest kid
in public school would be a better
option for my family. this would let me
see my family in Peru. have some saving to

What is your favorite charity and what do you do to support it?

Does my own family count?
I have helped then beyond my
financial limits.
- my husband usually donate to St. Jude
- I Volunteer for CASA awhile ago, wish I could do it
again.

What lessons have you learned about money and wealth?

→ Do not spent more than what
you have.
→ Built up your savings for the unexpected

Other aspects of money and wealth you would like to share with others or would like to hear more about from others...

How much should we give to the church? Is there any "acceptable porcentage"? What if I have debts, should I pay my debts first, and then ~~contr~~ donate to the church?

Reflection: Money & wealth
For your quiet reflection following group sharing.

What have I learned about myself while reflecting on and sharing thoughts about money and wealth?

How have my thoughts about money and wealth changed?

I was inspired by these stories or ideas shared by others:

What changes will I make in my decisions about my own wealth
and how I share God's gifts with others? Why?

_____

_____

_____

_____

What values will continue to influence how I and my family
approach money and wealth?

_____

_____

_____

_____

Resources
Resources I would like to share or that others have shared with me:

_____

_____

_____

_____

_____

God's Call
Through Life's Milestones

Light a candle

Opening prayer

Discernment Prayer
Walk with me, good and loving God, as I journey through life.
May I take your hand and be led by your Holy Spirit.
Fill me, inspire me, free me to respond generously to your call.
For I believe you desire my deepest joy,
and it is only in your company
that my soul will be satisfied
and my life will find its meaning and purpose.
Amen.
    —Sisters of Notre Dame

"The LORD came and revealed his presence, calling out as
before, 'Samuel, Samuel!' Samuel answered, 'Speak, for your
servant is listening.'" 1 Samuel 3:10 NAB

"God called out to him from the bush, 'Moses! Moses!' He answered, 'Here I am.' But the LORD said, 'I have witnessed the affliction of my people in Egypt and have heard their cry of complaint against their slave drivers, so I know well what they are suffering. Therefore I have come down to rescue them from the hands of the Egyptians and lead them out of that land into a good and spacious land, a land flowing with milk and honey... Come, now! I will send you to Pharaoh to lead my people, the Israelites, out of Egypt.' But Moses said to God, 'Who am I that I should go to Pharaoh and lead the Israelites out of Egypt?' He answered, 'I will be with you...'"
Exodus 3: 4, 7-8, 10-12 NAB

"As Jesus was walking beside the Sea of Galilee, he saw two brothers, Simon called Peter and his brother Andrew. They were casting a net into the lake, for they were fishermen. 'Come, follow me,' Jesus said, 'and I will make you fishers of men.' At once they left their nets and followed him. Going on from there, he saw two other brothers, James son of Zebedee and his brother John. They were in a boat with their father Zebedee, preparing their nets. Jesus called them, and immediately they left the boat and their father and followed him." Matthew 4: 18-22 NIV

The Bible gives us many wonderful examples of God's call: to Samuel, Moses, Jonah, Mary, the first disciples. In each, the calling is not an easy one and God continues to call them in different ways as they live their lives. In the same way, God calls us. And his call may evolve, change, or expand throughout our life as we are ready and willing to take on more or different service. Our talents, interests, and life experiences help prepare us for his work. We live out our calling in new ways as we mature and better understand the gifts God has given us. It can be difficult, as life changes around us, to know which callings are from God and which are expectations placed on us by ourselves or those around us.

As you reflect on the questions in this chapter, consider times you've been sure of God's calling for you as well as those times you wondered, perhaps anxiously, what might come next. What special gifts has the Spirit shared with you? How has your use of those gifts evolved with God's calling throughout the milestones of your life?

A unique journey

> "Then I heard the voice of the Lord, saying, 'Whom shall I send? Who will go for us?'" Isaiah 6:8 NAB

Who am I at this point in my life? How would I describe myself?

_____

_____

_____

_____

I believe right now in my life God is calling me to:

_____

_____

_____

Special talents or experiences God has given me to prepare me for this calling:

_____

_____

_____

"Certainly there are some calls that are lived over a lifetime, including the call to priesthood, religious life, marriage, and being a parent. For those calls and other calls to ministry, Catholic tradition says we must always look at who we are (how God created us as individuals with our gifts and talents), and what the needs are of the world around us."
—Fr. Tom Walker

Reflecting on life's milestones

At different points in our lives, God may call us to serve in different ways. Some people are called to vocations in single life, married life, or religious life. Some are called to be parents while others are not. We may work different jobs, volunteer in different places, and so on.

Family milestones

Our family vocation changes as we move from childhood to young adulthood and through our adult life. Underline all the family milestones you've reached and circle your current vocation(s):

single life	marriage	widow	religious life
mother	grandmother	great-grandmother	
sister	aunt	adult child caring for parents	

Paula, age 37, would like to be a mom but is having trouble getting pregnant. Janice, age 44, would like to be married but hasn't found the right partner. "Does that mean God doesn't intend this for me? How much of this is our choice?"

What I love about my current family vocation:

_____

_____

_____

A challenge of my current family vocation:

_____

_____

In addition to my biological family, I have a family of friends. How is my role in that family different than or similar to my traditional family?

_____

_____

Motherhood

The joys, challenges, and calling of motherhood changes with each child and throughout that child's life.

How many children I have:

Ages of my children:

infant   toddler   school age   teen   adult

How being a mother has changed my calling and how it continues to change as my children grow and mature:

....

....

....

....

When Heather's children were young, she taught Faith Formation. Then she became a volunteer for teen CYO. "I was called to different ministries as my children grew."

Aging

As we age and mature, we gain wisdom and refine talents that, combined with our life experiences, help us to be more compassionate and to respond to God's call in new ways. We also take on new health challenges, different responsibilities, and changes in independence that sometimes limit the ministries in which we can serve.

In what ways has my growing older affected what God asks me to do and how I am able to respond?

....

....

....

....

Life-changing events

Experiencing an event in our lives such as a death, birth, illness, an accident, a special friendship, a trip, or a job can impact the way we look at our lives, our choices, and our relationship with God.

A life-changing event that influenced the way I view my life, my relationship with God, or my calling:

_____

_____

_____

_____

Work

Throughout our lives, we make choices about how we contribute our talents. Circle work experiences you've had:

own a business   job(s) at other companies or organizations
homemaker   civic role
volunteer   other work:

How have my past work experiences added to my ability to do God's work?

_____

_____

_____

In what ways is my current career choice or ministry connected to my calling from God?

_____

_____

_____

_____

Community involvement

As we cross milestones in our lives, we become members of various communities. What ministries do you serve in your communities?

Civic community: military service, political service, voter/delegate, public health and safety, parks and recreation, fundraiser...

School community: volunteer, teacher, tutor, coach, school board, parent-teacher organization...

Church community: Eucharistic minister, catechist, liturgist, choir, parish council, education, adoration...

Larger community: mission trips, soup kitchens, food shelves, housing projects, mentoring...

Other communities and ministries:

_____

_____

_____

Ways God's call for me has changed over time in my communities:

_____

_____

_____

Ongoing discernment

As we continue to travel through the milestones of our life, continue to age, take on different family responsibilities, and become more aware of the needs in our communities, we continue to discern how God's call may be changing or evolving for us. Take a moment to reflect on how you discovered what God was asking of you throughout your past milestones. What are some ways you can continue to hear God as you go forward?

Learning from the past

Where have I found the most meaning in my life? Has there been a time I felt sure I was doing God's work? What signs confirmed for me I was on the right path?

_____

_____

_____

Was there a time I didn't understand or want what I felt God was calling me to do?

_____

_____

_____

Can I say no to God? What helps me say yes the first time God asks?

_____

_____

_____

When have I had to leave a ministry behind because of a new calling—how did I know it was time for a change?

_____

_____

_____

My talents and interests

What talents and interests have come back to me at different points in my life or have always been there, even if in the background?

_____

_____

_____

_____

As I've reached milestones, what are new ways I've learned to use those talents or pursue those interests?

_____

_____

_____

Matching needs

When I look around me today in my faith community and neighborhood, what needs match my interests and talents?

_____

_____

_____

_____

What can I handle in addition to my call to love and serve the Lord and my family?

_____

_____

_____

Does a lack of interest, a lack of need, or a lack of time indicate I need to leave doing a certain ministry? What factors do I consider when I notice the needs around me and decide whether or not I am the right person to step up?

_____

_____

_____

How far reaching?

We each touch many more lives than we realize. Some people are called to serve in their immediate families and in their parishes. Some are called to work in their greater community, even internationally. Reflect on your own awareness of how far your service reaches.

Am I comfortable with how far my current service reaches? Have I had thoughts about expanding my reach?

_____

_____

_____

What organizations or causes have captured my interest? What stops me from pursuing this?

_____

_____

_____

Is it God's voice or someone else's?

What expectations do others have of me? How does this affect where I place my energy and talents? Is this in communion with or working against what I feel God wants me to do?

_____

_____

_____

Ways I talk with God or listen to hear what he is asking of me:

_____

_____

_____

God, here are some questions I have about what you want me to do for you:

_____

_____

_____

> *"Every time we say yes to God we will get a little more sensitive to hearing him the next time."*
> — *John Ortberg,* God is Closer Than You Think

Trusting God

"For we walk by faith, not by sight." 2 Corinthians 5:7 NAB

Sometimes we get anxious when we're contemplating our next step or facing a challenging situation. (Should I marry him? How do I go on without him? Should I quit my job? Should we have children now? How will we afford this? Am I using my talents in a meaningful way?) We want to know ahead of time how things will turn out.

A decision, life milestone, or challenging situation that has caused or is now causing me stress or anxiety:

_____

_____

_____

Even Jesus was called
by God to the greatest
trial. Jesus prayed at
Gesthemane for the
cup to be taken just as
we sometimes pray to
ask that we will not
have to bear our cross.
Let us answer as
Jesus answered:
"Not my will, but
Thy will be done."

What helped/would help me feel better about this situation?

_____

_____

What about this situation was/am I most worried about?

_____

_____

What are some ways I can entrust these worries to God?

_____

_____

_____

Closing prayer

Heavenly Father, you have given me talents, interests, and life experiences that make me uniquely suited to answer your personal call, a call that changes throughout my life. Help me see the importance of my service in the lives I touch while doing your work. Send me encouragement when I am unsure of myself. Walk with me when the way is hard. Reassure me when I am worried about the way it will turn out. Humbly as your servant, I say "Yes." Amen.

Suggested topics and questions for group discussion

Use this space to prepare your own thoughts or to make notes during your group discussion.

Describe yourself at this point in your life. What is God calling you to do? What special gifts or talents have prepared you to answer?

How has your calling changed throughout your life? Where have you found the most meaning in your life? Is there a life changing event that influenced your relationship with God?

How do you know when it is God who is calling you? Have you ever said no? Tell us about your struggles and confirmations of God's call.

Other aspects of God's call through life's milestones you would like to share with others or would like to hear more about from others...

Reflection: God's call through life's milestones
For your quiet reflection following group sharing.

What I've learned about myself while reflecting on and sharing thoughts about ways God's call evolves or changes throughout life:

_____

_____

_____

I was inspired by these stories or ideas shared by others:

_____

_____

_____

What changes will I make in the way I listen for God's call? Why?

_____

_____

_____

What will I keep about my process of discernment?

_____

_____

_____

Resources
Resources I would like to share or that others have shared with me:

_____

_____

life balance

Mind - Body - Spirit Connections

Light a candle

Opening prayer

Jesus, please help me pay attention to the needs of my body, mind, heart, and spirit so I may use the gifts you've given me and respond positively and lovingly to all the demands of my daily life. Amen.

> "Or do you not know that your body is a temple of the Holy Spirit who is in you, whom you have from God, and that you are not your own?" 1 Corinthians 6:19 NASB

Often we think of life balance as managing all our obligations, tasks, and commitments. We are constantly juggling the amount of work we have to do with the amount of time we get to spend playing or the time we have left for our own needs. The resulting stress causes us to feel out of balance. But like many aspects of our life, balance begins within ourselves, not just from warding off all the pressures around us.

Living a healthy spiritual life requires that inner balance. Focusing on our physical, mental, and emotional energy helps create that overall healthy connection with our inner spirit and can have lasting effects on our actions and decisions in all aspects of our lives, including how well we tackle other life balance decisions.

Consider times you feel well balanced compared with times you feel stressed. What is different about your physical, mental, and emotional energy at those times? How does a good mind-body-spirit connection affect your life balance?

Ways my life feels well balanced right now:

_____

_____

_____

Ways my life feels out of balance right now:

_____

_____

_____

Assessing my health

On a scale of 1 (least healthy) to 5 (most healthy), this is how I feel about my health right now:

Physical health

(body weight, hair, skin, eyesight, hearing, muscle strength, endurance, fitness, energy level)

UNHEALTHY 1   2   3   4   5 HEALTHY

_____

_____

Mental health
(learning, thinking, awareness, memory, creativity, problem solving, curiosity)

UNHEALTHY 1   2   3   4   5 HEALTHY

Emotional health
(happy, satisfied, safe, trusting, loving, passionate, peaceful, high self-esteem, resilient, optimistic, sense of humor)

UNHEALTHY 1   2   3   4   5 HEALTHY

Spiritual health
(answering God's call, feeling close to God, using the gifts of the Spirit, regular worship, living as a Christian)

UNHEALTHY 1   2   3   4   5 HEALTHY

Trying times
When our inner health is well balanced, we are able to thoughtfully respond rather than simply react. Instead of yelling in the heat of the moment, we are able to take a moment to calmly respond with love and compassion and justice.

Times I have less patience:

Times I give too much to others and not enough to myself:

_____

_____

Times I feel jealous of someone else's choice for balance:

_____

_____

Times I feel tired, hungry, or restless:

_____

_____

Times I feel less equipped to handle stress, the unexpected, or conflict:

_____

_____

Are my basic needs met at these times? What can I change to better equip myself for these times?

_____

_____

Routines for getting the basics

We all have basic physical needs—exercise, healthy food, sleep—that need to be met every day. Those things affect how well we think and respond, how we handle a situation, and how quickly we'll cry about it. Good, healthy routines help us stay on a well-balanced path.

My favorite forms of exercise:

_____

_____

My exercise schedule:

_____

_____

Ways I make it easy for myself to make healthy food choices:

_____

_____

What mealtimes are like in our house:

_____

_____

My sleep schedule:

_____

_____

Things I do in my nightly routine that help me get ready for a good night's sleep:

_____

_____

What helps me or prevents me from maintaining the exercise, eating, and sleeping routines and habits that keep me physically balanced:

_____

_____

Maintaining a strong heart and mind
Our hearts and minds also have basic daily needs: positive thoughts, connections with caring people, and strategies to cope with difficult times.

In what ways do I regularly feed my mind with positive thoughts, reliable information, a loving perspective, and good coping strategies?

_____

_____

What daily inspirations help me stay positive?

_____

_____

What do I do to ensure I regularly surround myself with loving, caring people?

_____

_____

How do I help myself make positive choices about potentially harmful coping habits such as smoking or drinking alcohol?

_____

_____

Christine bakes to relieve stress. Meagan writes letters in a journal when she's angry. Ann makes a list of things that need to be done to help get them off her mind.

What are some healthy ways I respond to stressful situations?

_____

_____

When my mind is full of all the things I have to do and need to remember, what are some ways I clear the clutter?

_____

_____

Spiritual renewal

Taking care of our basic physical and emotional needs opens up our minds and bodies and hearts to receive Jesus. There are many ways in our religious rituals that we already make the connection of physically, mentally, and emotionally preparing ourselves to receive grace. For example, by not eating an hour before receiving Eucharist, we prepare our bodies and spirits to feel hungry for Jesus. By mentally reflecting on our sins before receiving Reconciliation, we open our hearts and spirits to receive God's forgiving grace. In the same way, our daily preparations for healthy bodies, minds, and hearts help prepare us for renewing our spirits as the center of our lives. And meeting a few spiritual basic needs each day helps us keep our bodies, minds, and hearts on the right track.

Meditation

Everyone meditates. Meditation is simply the process of letting your mind dwell with some intensity over a thought or image for a period of time. By choosing to meditate on positive thoughts, we help calm our mind and lift our spirits.

What is a favorite Bible verse, prayer, inspirational saying, or other positive mantra I could repeat to myself to help me think positively?

Where is a quiet place and when is a quiet time that I can clear my mind of negative thoughts and dwell on the positive?

"Spirituality is the sacred center out of which all life comes, including Mondays and Tuesdays and rainy Saturday afternoons in all their mundane and glorious detail....The spiritual journey is the soul's life commingling with ordinary life."
— *Christina Baldwin,*
Life's Companion

What are some ways I can take the most stressful times of my day, the times I find myself reacting instead of responding, and bring a quiet, positive peace to the moment?

_____

_____

_____

> Do you have the patience to wait
> till your mud settles and the water is clear?
> Can you remain unmoving
> till the right action arises by itself?
> —Lao-Tzu, *Tao Te Ching*

Spiritual food

Our souls need to eat each day, too. Choosing good soul food can make our spirits strong and ready to face whatever else the day brings.

How often do I read the Bible and how do I go about it?

_____

_____

_____

What do I get out of attending Mass on Sunday? What is my favorite part? What makes it difficult for me sometimes to glean a message for the week?

_____

_____

_____

_____

How does the Eucharist—received both at Communion at the Mass and through Christ in those around me—give me grace to face the challenges in my life?

_____

_____

_____

Who in my life has a great spiritual center? How often do I talk with this person?

_____

_____

What are some other ways I feed my soul?

_____

Each evening, Serena and her son read together a reflection from the daily Mass readings.

_____

Giving up the weight

"So humble yourselves under the mighty hand of God, that he may exalt you in due time. Cast all your worries upon him because he cares for you." 1 Peter 5:6-7 NAB

Sometimes our scales feel out of balance because our spirits are weighted down with our heavy cares and worries. We don't need to carry those burdens alone.

What are some burdens I can lay at Jesus' feet today?

_____

_____

_____

Who in my life can I rely on to help me when I have trouble giving my cares to God?

_____

_____

_____

Center of balance

By paying attention to the connections in our physical, mental, and spiritual health, we create the opportunity to find our center of balance.

Consider for a moment the first time trying yoga. You might be distracted by your image in the mirror, what the people around you are doing, or a technique the instructor is demonstrating. When you pay attention to all those other things, you can lose your balance. But when you learn to concentrate only on your own body and block out all the noise of the world, that's when your body and mind and spirit all work together. You could be on top of a mountain, at a beach, or in a gym at the YMCA. It won't matter. You are focused on your own center. The more you practice focusing on only that center, the more you are able to use this technique at other times of your day.

Being present

Practicing mindfulness can help us be truly present no matter what we're doing. Pay attention to the way food smells and tastes. When you are exercising, pay attention to each muscle you are working, to the pace of your heartbeat, to the way your body is flowing as you breathe. Every once in a while throughout your day, focus only on your breathing. We get so used to doing so many things at a time we can forget how much simply breathing a steady calm rhythm can wipe away anxiety, restore our perspective, and help us focus on what's important.

At the times of my day I feel the most balanced, what am I doing? What's happening around me and how do I respond to it? Is there anything I do to consciously keep myself balanced at those times?

_____

_____

_____

_____

How can I recreate that balance when I need it at other times of the day?

_____

_____

_____

When I feel the craziest, what is happening around me? What am I doing? What are others doing?

_____

_____

_____

_____

There are 1440 minutes in a day. I can spend an hour on myself and still have plenty for everyone else. When I focus on myself first, I have the positive energy and perspective to serve God and nurture and support my loved ones.

Are there responsibilities I put ahead of taking care of myself?

_____

_____

_____

Closing prayer

Lord, you give me a body as your temple. Guide me to make good choices about how I care for my body. You give me my daily bread. Teach me to taste and eat healthy foods with great joy and purpose. You give me a mind to think and a heart to feel. Let me experience all the emotions you bless me with yet manage them wisely. You give me the ability to use my body, mind, heart, and spirit in a healthy way to bring your strength and love into my daily life. Help me to be mindful and present in the moment so I can consciously live and act as a good Christian. In thanksgiving, I will take good care of myself so that you may remain the center of my life and in being so centered on you, I will find life's balance. Amen.

Suggested topics and questions for group discussion
Use this space to prepare your own thoughts or to make notes during your group discussion.

How do you feel about your overall health? In what ways or at what times does your life feel well balanced or out of balance?

What daily routines and choices help you maintain positive, healthy habits? How do you manage transitions, stress, and other obstacles?

In what ways do you feed your soul?

_____

_____

_____

_____

Other aspects of mind-body-spirit connections you would like to share with others or would like to hear more about from others...

_____

_____

_____

_____

Reflection: Mind-body-spirit connections
For your quiet reflection following group sharing.

What have I learned about myself while reflecting on and sharing thoughts about how my physical, mental, and emotional health is connected to my spiritual health?

_____

_____

_____

I was inspired by these stories or ideas shared by others:

_____

_____

_____

What changes will I make in my daily priorities to create more balance? Why?

_____

_____

_____

_____

What about my daily routine will I keep the same?

_____

_____

_____

_____

Resources

Resources I would like to share or that others have shared with me:

_____

_____

_____

_____

_____

Reflections

Light a candle

Opening prayer
Lord, thank you for the circle of women you have brought into my life.
Thank you for the time and opportunity to reflect on the topics in this
journal. Help me continue to carve out time in my week to reflect on
ways I live my faith in my daily life. Encourage me to get to know you
better through my personal prayer, to share my beliefs in our family
rituals and traditions, to see Jesus in my relationships, to put my lessons
from my spiritual role models into action, to be a good steward of the
wealth you entrust to me, to listen for your call at all stages of my life,
and to take good care of my body, mind, heart, and spirit so I may be
eager and ready to do your will. Amen.

Personal reflection
Go back through your journal and review your responses. Read the
reflections you wrote after your group discussions. Take a few moments
in a calm and quiet place to simply let this overall experience settle in
your mind. As you reflect in this last chapter, consider ways your opinion
or understanding has changed. Do you know yourself better? Do you

have ideas for how to bring your faith more readily into your daily life? How has the Spirit guided you in recent weeks? In what ways have you already grown closer to God?

My initial thoughts about this experience:

_____

_____

_____

The topics that most resonated with me:

_____

_____

_____

The questions that were most difficult for me to answer:

_____

_____

_____

What I've learned about myself or my family while journaling:

_____

_____

_____

New things I've learned about the Catholic faith:

_____

_____

_____

Ways my faith has deepened through reflection and group sharing:

_____

_____

_____

Stories and ideas that have stuck with me:

_____

_____

_____

_____

_____

Changes I will make because of this experience:

_____

_____

_____

Things I will keep the same because of this experience:

_____

_____

_____

Resources I would most like to read or know more about or
resources I'd like to share with my circle:

_____

_____

_____

Other topics I'd like to explore beyond this journal:

_____

_____

To prepare for your final circle discussion of this journal, consider
the personal reflection you just completed as well as your
reflections at the end of each chapter. Are there any revelations,
thoughts, or additional ideas would you like to share with your
group that you did not have a chance to in other discussions?

About prayer and my personal connection with God:

_____

_____

_____

About rituals and traditions for Catholic feast days and holidays:

_____

_____

_____

About seeing Jesus in my relationships:

_____

_____

_____

About my spiritual role models:

_____

_____

_____

About my values and beliefs about money and wealth:

_____

_____

About God's call for me throughout my life:

_____

_____

About the connections between my physical, mental, emotional, and spiritual health:

_____

_____

_____

About my overall experience and my personal reflections:

_____

_____

_____

Final group discussion

As your group meets for the final session, plan the atmosphere that best fits the personality of your group. For example, you might plan an intimate setting with time for a quiet reflection of each chapter. You might include time to share your responses from earlier in this Reflections chapter. Your group might also want a more social ending that celebrates the friendships created in the circle. If you'd like to focus on only a few questions for your final group discussion, consider the following questions.

Suggested topics and questions for group discussion
Use this space to prepare your own thoughts or to make notes during your group discussion.

What is one thing you learned about yourself or your faith during this time of journaling?

_____

_____

_____

What is one thing you are now inspired to change? Or one thing you are currently doing that has been affirmed by this experience?

_____

_____

_____

What aspect of this experience did you enjoy the most? The time you spent with yourself reflecting and journaling? The fellowship with other women? Something else?

_____

_____

_____

You have been exploring how you live your faith in your daily life. In what ways would you like to take that exploration a step further? Is there a topic that resonated with you or a new topic you thought of while journaling that you would like to learn more about? What will you look for next in your spiritual journey?

_____

_____

_____

_____

Do you have resources you'd like to share with the group or a resource you are looking for?

_____

_____

_____

_____

At the end of your meeting, gather together in a circle. Offer a petition of thanks:

Lord, thank you for the circle of women you have brought into my life. Thank you for encouraging me to take this time for myself. Thank you for guiding me on my personal journey.

Add your own prayer of thanksgiving:

_____

_____

_____

Together as a group read the poem "In the Circle" on the last page as a final closing prayer.

Closing prayer

In the Circle

I find myself
in the circle
having walked an open path

around and round
in peacefulness
within a labyrinth

with each step
my joys and tears
with other women shared

burdens lifted
on the journey
to the center where

I find myself
in the circle
I did not walk alone

sitting with me
here the Father
the Spirit, and the Son

together we
will journey out
a path I know so well

renewed in faith
with strength and love
I found here in the circle